The Postcard History of
DUBLIN

The Little
MUSEUM of
DUBLIN

TREVOR WHITE

The Little
MUSEUM of
DUBLIN

An Chomhairle Oidhreachta
The Heritage Council

The Postcard History of Dublin
By Trevor White
Design by Dara Flynn and Barbara Sangster
First Edition, published January 2023
Published by the Little Museum of Dublin
Produced with support from The Heritage Council

ISBN 978-1-7392315-0-7

For Marty White

"No city exists in the present tense, it is the only surviving mass-statement of our ancestors, and it changes inversely to its inhabitants. It is old when they are young, and when they grow old it has become amazingly and shiningly young again."

James Stephens

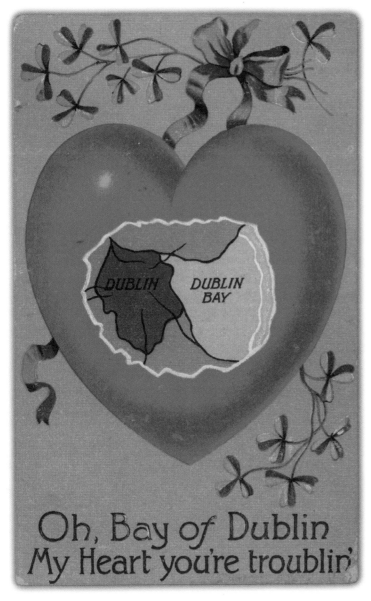

Oh, Bay of Dublin
My Heart you're troublin'

Every postcard is full of meaning. There is the stamp, of course; where the card was sent from; the destination; the picture often reflects the material culture of a place; and the message on either side may catch the heart off guard.

DUBLIN WAS AN IRISH VILLAGE, A VIKING TOWN and an English city. Today, it is the mass-statement of our ancestors, the capital of a mature democracy, a source of rural suspicion, and a fashionable city-break destination. Many of the people who visit the city will send a postcard to someone who occupies their thoughts. If you are loved, you may have received such a missive. If you are *in* love, you have probably sent one.

Postcards are not just a way to convey the tender longings of the heart. They were one of the most popular methods of communication for many years, and collecting postcards remains quite a common hobby. (I stumbled into this world after falling in love with a cute dog holding a newspaper.) The subject even has a very grand name: deltiology. This is not to pretend that we are talking about a branch of English literature.

THERE ARE GOOD REASONS why some art-lovers do not bother to collect postcards. There are concerns, for example, around authenticity and duplication. It is hard to know when certain postcards were printed, and sometimes they are copied in a way that does not flatter anyone. Decentralised and uncontrollable, the world of postcards is fascinating, but essentially unreliable. It sounds a bit like Irish history.

In Ireland, we pretend to have a monopoly on fun, but the market is more unsentimental than we imagine. If it flies, you can sell it anywhere.

One paradox of modern tourism is that the more visitors a place attracts, the less it is the unspoilt paradise that attracted them in the first place.

P OSTCARDS ARE A MINOR ART FORM. But they are certainly useful to historians. Our focus *here* is Dublin. The postcard could also serve as a lens for looking at many other subjects, such as nationalism, empire, modernity, emigration, tourism or the roles of women.

For example, the postcard on the left is an example of capitalism at its most enticing. *That* dog is why I bought Lot 11 in a Dublin auction house on May 13, 2015.

Dublin Postcard Albums

Two large albums of postcards relating mainly to Dublin
city and county, over 500 in all, monochrome and colour, some postally used,
some interesting cards, some real photographs.

Look at the loyalty in the eyes of that red setter.* As someone who likes writing, reading and watching dogs do funny tricks, I *needed* to buy that postcard. And even today, many years after receiving some news from Rustington, I think the collection was good value at €400.

We all make our own excuses.

*Or is it a cocker spaniel? Answers on a postcard to 15 St. Stephen's Green, D2.

THIS IS A BOOK ABOUT A COLLECTION OF POSTCARDS. Each one of them is a time capsule, full of florid information; declarations of high feeling; petty rebukes. *(Look at the grumpy head on Harry.)* Individually, these artefacts may be of limited interest. But for all the wounded pride, the bad weather and the travel plans, there is another side to every picture postcard. In this book, the images animate a high-speed adventure about the ups and downs of life in the Hibernian metropolis.

Here is an incomplete history of Dublin on the back of a postcard.*

*If this project has brevity as a guiding principle, that is because postcards are brief, and the reader is busy, but the goal is to make something fuller and more useful than a few scrawled words: history my children might read.

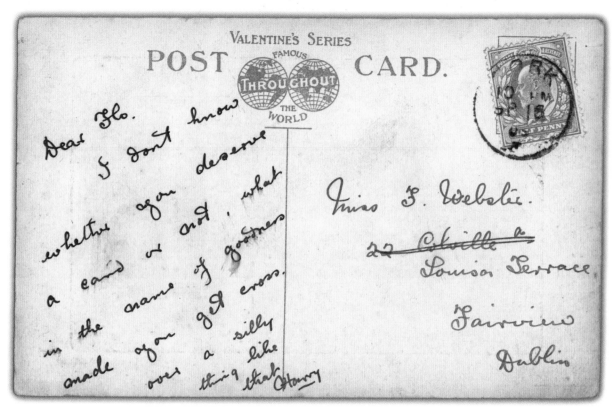

POST CARD.

FAMOUS THROUGHOUT THE WORLD

Dear Flo.

I dont know whether you deserve a card or not, what in the name of goodness made you get cross over a silly little thing like that. Harry

Miss F. Webster.

22 Colville a

Louisa Terrace

Fairview

Dublin

Harry appears to be digging a hole for himself.

History on a Postcard
The story of Dublin in fourteen images

The Chapel Royal The Castle

St. Stephen's Green, Dublin.

College Green, Dublin

Dublin. Custom House

Reading room
Royal Hospital, Dublin.

KING WILLIAM III CROSSING THE BOYNE
JULY 1st 1690. C.B.08

432 — 1932
SOUVENIR of the 1500 th. ANNIVERSARY
the COMING of ST. PATRICK to IRELAND

"Wait for me, darling!"

400

1600

1700

ST. PATRICK ARRIVES
432 AD

TRINITY COLLEGE IS
FOUNDED
1592

DUKE OF ORMOND
RETURNS TO DUBLIN
1662

BATTLE OF
THE BOYNE
1690

DUBLIN CASTLE
IS FOUNDED
1204

ST STEPHEN'S GREEN
IS ENCLOSED
1664

Dublin is founded
841

Battle of Clontarf
1014

Irish people evicted from
Dublin and settle at Irishtown
1454

First map of
Dublin drawn
1610

Penal Laws enacted
1695-1745

Is this her place among the nations of the earth?

Parnell's Monument, Dublin.

The Nation...

...osed grave of Robert Emmet a...

Dublin. Daniel O'Connell and many other noted men have lived in this famous square.

SACKVILLE STREET, DUBLIN.

The Quays from O'Connell's Bridge, After the Rebellion.

Grafton Street, Dublin, Ireland.

"Honey, you're history."

1800   1900   2000

GOLDEN AGE OF
DUBLIN
1750-1800

CATHOLIC
EMANCIPATION
1829

EASTER RISING
1916

MARY ROBINSON
ELECTED PRESIDENT
1990

ROBERT EMMET'S
REBELLION
1803

CHARLES STEWART
PARNELL DIES
1891

IRISH FREE STATE
1922

Guinness Brewery opens
at St. James's Gate
1759

Great Famine
1845-1851

Republic of Ireland
declared
1949

Celtic Tiger period
1995-2007

Christianity arrived on the island of Ireland in the fifth century A.D. when St. Patrick came as a slave from Britain.

I RELAND HAS BEEN CALLED THE ISLAND OF SAINTS AND SCHOLARS. It was Patrick, a Romano-British slave, who brought the word of God to the Irish. Today this mysterious missionary is remembered in the name of Dublin's most famous cathedral.

There were Celts in Ireland long before the Vikings arrived, and the Vikings who arrived in 841 A.D. were not the first Vikings, but they *were* the first to establish a town in Dublin.

By the end of the ninth century, Hiberno-Norse Dublin was a militarised community and a regional base for trading, raiding and slaving: a place of consequence in the northern imagination. The town would eventually become the largest Viking settlement outside Scandinavia.

THE GREATEST *faux pas* IN IRISH HISTORY was when an Irishman invited a foreigner to settle an argument. It happened in 1166, when the exiled king of Leinster, Dermot MacMurrough, asked for help from Henry II. The king gave permission for MacMurrough to hire some soldiers, and the Irishman convinced an Anglo-Norman mercenary, Strongbow, to assist his cause. The traitor MacMurrough even promised Strongbow the hand of his own daughter, Aoife, in marriage.

Strongbow arrived in 1170 – and he duly throttled the Irish, before Henry II came to Dublin and asserted his rule over Strongbow *and* Ireland. The king then published a charter conferring Dublin to the men of Bristol.

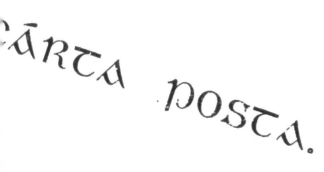

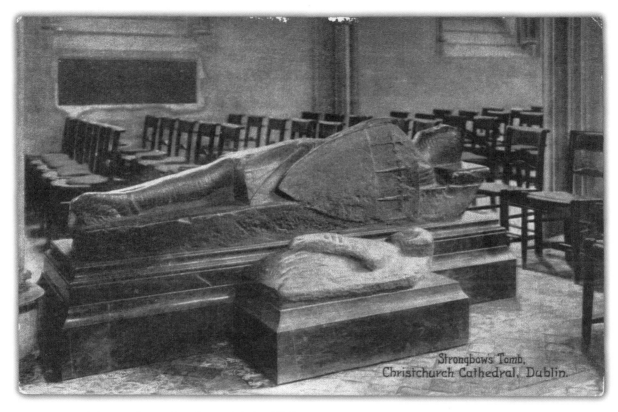

This postcard depicts Strongbow's tomb in Dublin's
Christchurch Cathedral: is it an example of dark tourism?

The Chapel Royal The Castle

Dublin 26/9/02

Trust this will be acceptable for your album. I know you like old places. Goodbye. Smiles.

"Trust this will be acceptable for your album. I know you like old places." Until quite recently, collecting postcards was a very popular hobby in many countries.

As the centre of England's first colony, Dublin became a place of shifting alliances, acute danger and something approaching normality. The lines of division were never as clearly drawn as pub historians imagine.*

The construction of Dublin Castle (from 1204) gave the project a forbidding face. But outside the castle, many people existed in the twilight zone between begging and scraping by. In the Middle Ages, this is a story about short lives and catastrophic misery. Famine and plague had disastrous effects – the Black Death arrived in August 1348 and killed 14,000 Dubliners by Christmas – but the city bounced back.

This is also a story about unlikely survival.

*The relationship between native and newcomer is complex, awkward and provisional: some marry each other; some kill each other; most people put up with each other for the sake of an easy life.

A POISONOUS FEUD ROCKED ENGLAND IN THE 1530S. Rejecting the authority of Rome, Henry VIII forcibly converted many of his subjects, but the Protestant faith never really took hold in Ireland – except where settlers from Scotland were transplanted to Ulster. In the sixteenth and seventeenth centuries, large swathes of Ireland were simply taken by the English state and doled out to servants of the new order.

The English Civil War was a continuation of the Reformation by other means, with two sides fighting for control of the English crown. In 1649, the Parliamentarians defeated a combined Royalist and Confederate force at Rathmines. Oliver Cromwell called the battle "an astonishing mercy" from God himself.

Who *was* this rogue?

College Green, Dublin

In 1592, Trinity College Dublin was opened in the name of Queen Elizabeth. Ireland's oldest university was a friend to the colonial project for over three hundred years.

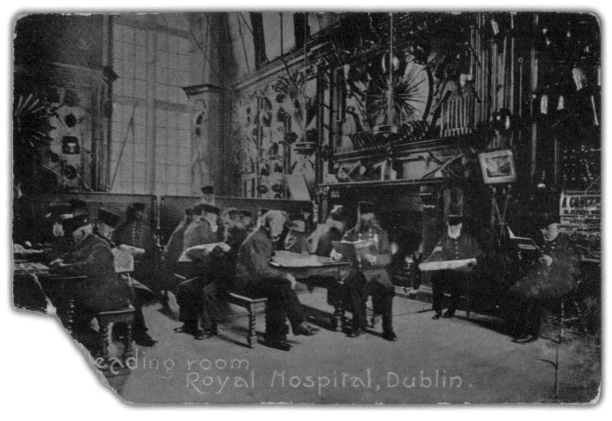

The Duke of Ormond founded the Royal Hospital in
Kilmainham, the oldest classical building in Ireland.
Inspired by Les Invalides in Paris, it served as an elegant
refuge for retired soldiers until 1927.

I N ENGLAND, OLIVER CROMWELL IS REGARDED AS A PROTO-DEMOCRAT, but he is not warmly remembered in Ireland. Why? Because he sent many Catholic families "to hell or Connacht", giving their land to new English settlers, and sanctioned the murder of up to a quarter of the Irish population. You would not want his picture around the house.

After Cromwell's death, the British monarchy was restored, and James Butler, Duke of Ormond, returned to Dublin in 1662 to serve in the newly restored position of viceroy. Ormond had spent time in exile at the French court, and in Paris he saw what good architecture and planning could do for a city and its self-esteem. Ormond is said to have brought the Renaissance to Ireland. He was certainly the first person to imagine the metropolis that Dublin might become.

In the right light, on a good day, the city still reflects his glory.

POSTAGE.

INLAND,
½d.
FOREIGN,
1d.

I N 1664, THE CITY ASSEMBLY CREATED A PARK, enabling the hard-up administration to sell off seventeen acres around St. Stephen's Green. The richest commoner in Ireland, William Petty, was among the early residents of the square. His widow, Baroness Shelburne, is remembered in the name of a grand hotel *(pictured on the right)* that stands on the site once occupied by their home.

The Green soon became a refuge for the social elite. A Cornish widow, Mrs Pendarves, arrived in Dublin in 1731. "I must say the environs are delightful," she wrote to a friend. "The town is bad enough, narrow streets and dirty-looking houses, but some good ones are scattered about; and as for Stephen's Green, I think it may be preferred to any square in London."

Like many Dubliners, I admit to having a soft spot for the Green.* Alongside Smithfield and Phoenix Park, this handsome refuge is a legacy of James Butler's rule. We continue to walk the Duke of Ormond's Dublin.

*One day my ashes will fertilise some plants. Join me for coffee at eleven.

Shelbourne Hotel, St. Stephen's Green, Dublin.

St. Stephen's Green, Dublin

TO WISH YOU
A HAPPY CHRISTMAS

"For Dublin can be heaven
With coffee at eleven,
And a stroll in Stephen's Green.
There's no need to hurry.
There's no need to worry.
You're the king and the lady's a queen."

Dublin Saunter

College Green.   Dublin.

Lawrence Publisher Dublin 5858

A statue of William III on College Green was the subject of frequent attacks, the most sincere form of art criticism. The statue was blown up by republicans in 1929.

I N 1690, THE PROTESTANT WILLIAM OF ORANGE BEAT the forces of the Catholic James II near Drogheda. A proxy fight for European supremacy, the Battle of the Boyne confirmed the Protestant Ascendancy for centuries to come. It also encouraged a strain of anti-Catholicism that made Anglo-Irish relations more toxic than ever before.

KING WILLIAM III CROSSING THE BOYNE
JULY 1TH 1690.

Conversely, Dublin became a place of refuge for Huguenots fleeing religious persecution in France. By 1720, at least five per cent of the residents spoke French. The Huguenots made the city a richer and more interesting place, but this is not to ignore the personality of Dublin itself. I like the phrase of the poet Louis MacNeice, who once described it as a place that appropriated "all the alien brought."

THE EIGHTEENTH CENTURY BEGINS WITH JONATHAN SWIFT, the Dean of St. Patrick's Cathedral, who wrote *Gulliver's Travels* and put Dublin on the literary map of the world.

Colonisation was a faltering process that operated in fits and starts. Sometimes the imperial project was unequivocally good for the demographics of Dublin. Between 1600 and 1800, the population grew from 10,000 to 200,000.

Towards the end of the eighteenth century, a corrupt, unrepresentative parliament on College Green reformed some of the most egregious anti-Catholic laws. Henry Grattan and other members of the parliament asserted 'Irish' rights, and the city acquired a surface patina of glamour.

Jonathan Swift made his name as a Tory propagandist in London, before returning to his birthplace to be Dean of St. Patrick's Cathedral. Swift used language in a revolutionary new way.

St.Patricks Cathedral.
Dublin.

DEKRVYFF

Merrion Square, Dublin. Daniel O'Connell and many other noted men have lived in this famous square.

THE IMPORTANCE OF BEING EARNEST

"I have the simplest tastes," wrote Oscar Wilde. "I am always satisfied with the best."

I N THE SO-CALLED GOLDEN AGE OF DUBLIN, a small group of architects built the nucleus of what *we* call Georgian Dublin.* Whole streets were rebuilt or swept away (by the powerful Wide Streets Commissioners) to accommodate notions of urban splendour. Consider, for example, this postcard view of Merrion Square. Here is a glimpse of privilege on a grand scale. When a young Catholic lawyer called Daniel O'Connell wanted to move up in the world, he sold his house on Westland Row and bought a mansion on the square.

Exactly fifty years later, an eye surgeon called William Wilde made the same short journey. William's son, Oscar, would confound his peers in Trinity College before dazzling strangers everywhere. Merrion Square is where Oscar Wilde learned to tie his shoelaces.

*The term 'Georgian Dublin' was invented in the twentieth century.

The Golden Age of Dublin

A city tries to look its best

The Four Courts, Dublin.

The Rotunda, Dublin. Situated at north end of Sackville Street

DAIL EIREANN, DUBLIN.

City Arms, Dublin.

MUSEUM, SCHOOL OF ART & NATIONAL LIBRARY, DUBLIN. Copyright EF&Co.

Botanic Gardens, Glasnevin.

ROTUNDA HOSPITAL, DUBLIN.

Four Courts, Dublin.

City Hall, Dublin.

Science and Art Museum, Dublin.

Old Houses of Parliament, Dublin.

Vice Regal Lodge, Dublin.

Valentines Series

CELEBRITY ARCHITECTS LIKE James Gandon built public buildings that greatly enhanced the urban streetscape. By the end of the eighteenth century, the Hibernian metropolis was the second city of the British Empire and the sixth largest city in Europe, with a population larger than Rome or Madrid. There was good reason to look forward to a new century of prosperity and growth.

What happened next?

The father of Irish republicanism, Theobald Wolfe Tone, *(pictured in the stamp above)* was caught fomenting rebellion against British rule in 1798. The government seized an opportunity, and the Dublin parliament was basically bribed into abolishing itself.

The 1800 Act of Union returned power to London. This prompted a middle and upper class exodus from Dublin. The cliché is that everything turned sour. Like most clichés, it contains a measure of truth, but it is easy to overstate the deprivation of post-Union Dublin.

Dublin. Custom House.

James Gandon's Custom House is Dublin's grandest public building, although the Loopline Bridge has stolen this wonderful view. The other pictures on this page give the reader a full measure of Gandon's genius.

In 1803, Robert Emmet led a botched city-centre *coup d'etat*.
His speech from the dock is a classic piece of oratory.

T HERE WAS ANOTHER REBELLION against British rule in 1803. It was led by 25-year-old Robert Emmet, who gave a heroic courtroom speech that Oscar Wilde would later recite in town halls all over America. That speech concluded with the words, "Let no man write my epitaph. When my country takes her place among the nations of the earth, then, *and not till then*, let my epitaph be written." According to Wilde, nothing had quite the same effect on Irish-American audiences.

CATHOLIC IRELAND FOUND A VOICE in Daniel O'Connell. This Kerry-born lawyer secured Catholic emancipation in 1829, winning the right for Catholics to sit in the London parliament.

O'Connell led the campaign to open Glasnevin cemetery, where both Catholics and Protestants could be buried, and in 1841 the City Council elected its first Catholic Lord Mayor in O'Connell himself. So here is a man who properly looms over Dublin. His statue on O'Connell Street (formerly Sackville Street) is the subject of many topographical postcards.

* The City of the Dead is the final resting place for over 1.5 million people. O'Connell's remains lie in a crypt beneath the tallest round tower in Ireland.

SACKVILLE STREET, DUBLIN.

Raphael Tuck & Sons "County" Postcard No. 2940. Co. Dublin
Phototype in

This is another of the cards you are wanting — When the competition is over I may be able to complete some sets for you as there are many duplicates among the thousands I have. a.m.b

Opinion is split on the question of text. Some deltiologists prefer to collect unwritten postcards.

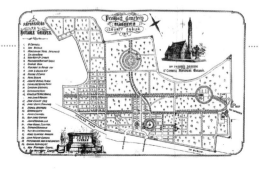

Did you know that bloodhounds used to guard this cemetery?

In Ireland, the reality of mass starvation is traditionally represented by emptiness; absence; silence.

I N FEBRUARY, 1847, DANIEL O'CONNELL BEGGED THE GOVERNMENT TO save the starving poor of Ireland. It was his last speech in the House of Commons, and O'Connell had the weight of a nation on his shoulders. But the English were not listening.

The Great Famine of 1845–1852 was the worst famine in Europe in the nineteenth century. It claimed the lives of one million Irish people, and another two million were forced to emigrate.* However, the population of Dublin actually increased during the Famine, as many victims poured into the city. It was not the first wave of outsiders – there had been Vikings, Anglo-Normans, Huguenots, Quakers and many others – but these rural newcomers were especially beleaguered. Their experience at the hands of a remote British government would encourage the claims of nationalists.

Ireland must be free.

*In 2021, Ireland's population exceeded 5m for the first time since the Famine.

ALL GREAT CITIES BOUNCE BACK. And immigrants are typically part of that story. In the 1870s, another group of newcomers arrived in Dublin from Lithuania. This small community of Litvak Jews established a lively presence around Portobello. By the mid-1940s, there were five thousand Jewish people living in (or near) Little Jerusalem.*

Dublin was a place of burgeoning Catholic power in the nineteenth century. While the city had few major industries to speak of, there were improvements in urban governance. And the development of the North Bull Wall provided an enduring solution to the problems of Dublin Port. (In certain wind conditions, ships could not reach the city for several weeks at a time and shipwrecks were common.) This era also saw the foundation of Dublin Zoo – one of the oldest in the world – and the opening of the world's first commuter railway line, from Westland Row to Kingstown.

Welcoming the arrival of the typewriter and the telephone, Victorian Dublin was also an early adopter of the postcard.

*Today the area is home to a large Muslim population.

Zoological Gardens Phoenix Park Dublin.

Dublin Zoo was opened in 1831. A flag-waving project for the British Empire, the zoo has always occupied a moral grey zone, despite its popularity.

The history of postcards is full of claim and counter-claim,
but "Greetings from Scarborough" has proper clout.

T HE FIRST POSTCARDS WERE just a plain piece of cardboard with an imprinted halfpenny stamp. There was no picture, the medium waiting for a small but crucial fix.

The first picture postcard in Britain *("Greetings from Scarborough", left)* was made in 1894. The medium would eventually become full colour, and the period around the turn of the twentieth century is known as the *Golden Age of Postcards*.* Millions of people were introduced to the compact pleasure of sending and receiving a postcard; the act, that is, of measuring the gap between where I write and where you read.

Here was a cheap, mass-produced form of communication that enabled ordinary people to express their deepest and most banal fantasies, to record an affection, or just to boast about where they went on holidays.

What could be more democratic?

*William Mervin Lawrence was the Irish postcard king. A marketing genius, Lawrence cornered the market in topographical views, including numerous examples in this book. Much of the credit should also go to his employee, Robert French, who took over 30,000 of the photographs that are now to be found in the Lawrence Collection in the National Photographic Archive. This is a peerless visual record of life in Ireland.

I N THE 1870S, A LANDOWNER CALLED CHARLES STEWART PARNELL
campaigned for Home Rule, a limited form of independence.
After putting the Irish Question at the centre of British politics,
Parnell's career ended in disgrace because of a divorce scandal. A victim
of religious rectitude, he died a year later, at the age of forty-five, and
his death turned a generation of radicals against parliamentary politics.
Today, Charles Stewart Parnell is remembered as a hero of constitutional
nationalism. He stands at the top of O'Connell Street, reminding passersby
that "No man has the right to fix a boundary to the march of a nation."

Standing nineteen metres tall, the Parnell monument salutes the greatest leader of the late nineteenth century.

Parnell's Monument, Dublin.

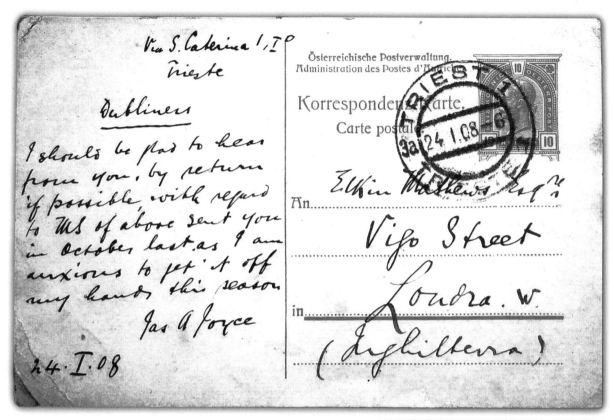

Via S. Caterina 1, I°
Trieste

Dubliners

I should be glad to hear
from you, by return
if possible, with regard
to MS of above sent you
in October last. as I am
anxious to get it off
my hands this season
                    Jas A Joyce

24. I. 08

Österreichische Postverwaltung.
Administration des Postes d'Autriche

Korrespondenzkarte.
Carte postale

An...... Elkin Mathews Esq™

Vigo Street

Londra. W.

in _____

(Inghilterra)

In *Ulysses*, Joyce made the supreme novel of the twentieth century, but it was not even his first masterpiece. That honour belongs to *Dubliners*, the greatest collection of short stories in the English language. It was rejected by publishers 22 times.

DUBLIN HORSE SHOW, 1904.
THE JUDGES' STAND.

DUBLIN WAS A SMALL, WELL-BEHAVED CITY on 16 June 1904, the day when James Joyce first walked out with Nora Barnacle.* Joyce's portrait of the city on that date is a landmark in the cultural life of Ireland and Europe.

In *Ulysses*, Joyce created a portrait that is microscopic in detail and wildly virtuosic. Writing in Zurich, Trieste and Paris, Joyce caught the conversation of Dublin from afar. His ear was sensitive to the rhythms of the urban pageant, to joy and regret, the power of the quotidian, the small number of slights that sustain a life.

A hundred years after the publication of Joyce's masterpiece, we recognise *Ulysses* as the first real expression of Dublin's potential: to become the capital of a dynamic European republic.

*James Joyce sang in a concert at the Dublin Horse Show in 1904.

IN 1907, DUBLIN MADE AN EXHIBITION of itself for six months, when nearly three million people visited a world's fair in what is today called Herbert Park. Backed by the most prominent tycoon of his day – William Martin Murphy – the highlights of the International Exhibition included a reproduction of a Somali village, with a group of people imported from British Somaliland. (Today, we see such events within a broader agenda to commodify and sensationalise subjugated peoples.) But there were also more innocent pleasures to be had in the exhibition, including a water chute that enabled visitors to look down their noses at Ballsbridge. *What japes!* The pond at the bottom of the chute still survives.

The Exhibition was a flag-waving exercise for the British Empire and a tourism bonanza. It was also the first major event in Dublin that was made for the souvenir postcard.

Writing to her beloved from Dublin, a woman says she visits the Exhibition every day. "I must take you on the Helter Skelter." It feels like a naughty afterthought.

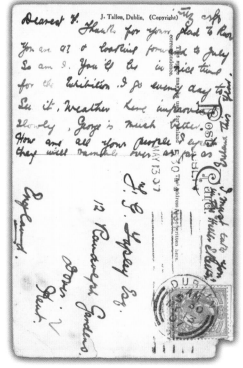

IRISH INTERNATIONAL EXHIBITION. DUBLIN. 1907
THE WATER CHUTE.

Another for *the Collection.*

Irish International Exhibition, Dublin, 1907. *Main Entrance* *(Copyright)*

IRISH INTERNATIONAL EXHIBITION, 1907.
LANDING STAGE FROM WATER CHUTE.

IRISH INTERNATIONAL EXHIBITION, 1907.—LAKE AND FINE ART GALLERY

Irish International Exhibition Dublin 1907
The Somali Village

IRISH INTERNATIONAL EXHIBITION, DUBLIN, 1907.—GENERAL VIEW FROM ART GALLERY
(Copyright)

IRISH INTERNATIONAL EXHIBITION, 1907.—CONCERT HALL

IRISH INTERNATIONAL EXHIBITION, 1907.—VIEW FROM DONNYBROOK ENTRANCE

Irish International Exhibition, Dublin, 1907   Some of the Side Shows
Copyright

THE OLD AGE PENSION WAS INTRODUCED TO IRELAND IN 1909. This civic benison transformed the lives of many people in Edwardian Dublin. Postcards from the period demonstrate the humour, pride and priggishness of Irish society. They lie to us in full colour. The city had the highest infant mortality rate of any city in these islands.

KINGSTOWN HARBOUR CO., DUBLIN.

TO KINGSTOWN.

The people here in Kingstown are so hospitable, that there is hardly anything they wont do, to ensure one having a good time.

Aug 18th

POST CARD.

Dear May i received your letter quite safe also the papers Dear May i am quite well trusting you are the same i shall be going to Dublin to morrow Monday to a polo match at Phoenix Park with the car

A young man fixes a date in 1907. Straddling two spaces, from where I write to where you read, the postcard is a bridge-builder that keeps relationships in good repair.

THE BIGGEST INDUSTRIAL RELATIONS DISPUTE IN IRISH HISTORY started in August, 1913, when tram-workers put down their badges and began a strike that would become known as the Dublin Lockout. It was a demonstration of weakness, as the trams were moving again within forty minutes. What followed was unbridled class warfare, as two opposing sides led by egomaniacs (union leader Jim Larkin and tycoon William Martin Murphy) were mediated by a distant and preoccupied British government. The striking men were effectively starved back to work.

What was the answer to the Irish Question? Home Rule – a limited form of independence from Britain – seemed plausible and, eventually, attainable. But the First World War diverted the attention of the British government. Over 200,000 Irishmen served in the British forces during the war. About 35,000 lost their lives.

A tourist corresponds from Bray to Dublin in 1915: "Having a ripping time... while writing this Maggie is washing her feet in the [Powerscourt] waterfall." The image and the message make Wicklow seem even more exotic than it is today.

The Gardens, Bray

AN OLD ADAGE SAYS THAT England's difficulty is Ireland's opportunity, but the relationship has never been that simple. When Irish rebels launched an armed insurrection in 1916, many of them had a second-hand memory of the Famine, while others also had intimate connections to the enemy. Rebel leader James Connolly spoke with a Scottish accent. Patrick Pearse's father was English.

The Easter Rising was the most successful failure in Irish history. Six years later, the Irish secured their independence. To put it another way: the six-day rebellion was the formative act in the struggle for freedom. "All changed, changed utterly," wrote William Butler Yeats,

"A terrible beauty is born."

Most of the 485 people killed in the Easter Rising were civilians. Forty were children. There is nothing pretty about the birth of the Irish state, but this is not unusual: most countries begin in violence.

*To be clear, this was not an all-male fight. Many of the people who took part that week were women, such as Constance Markievicz and Margaret Skinnider, who both fought at St. Stephen's Green.

The Quays from O'Connell's Bridge, Dublin.
(After the Rebellion)

After the Insurrection.—West side of Lr. Sackville St., showing Ruins of Hotel Metropole.

The aftermath of the Easter Rising is captured in titillating portraits of destruction. Travelling to places that are associated with death or tragedy is a social phenomenon with its own literature. Dark tourism is for strong stomachs.

The RMS Leinster was sunk by a German submarine in October 1918, a month before the end of the war. The loss of the mail boat left 501 people dead, including c.300 soldiers and nurses returning to the front. It was the worst disaster in Irish maritime history.

THE UNREPENTANT IRISH NATIONALISTS would keep fighting the British. After a landslide victory in the 1918 election, they launched a two-year guerrilla war of independence. In the autumn of 1921, Michael Collins, Arthur Griffith and three others were sent to London to negotiate on behalf of the Irish. They were successful... in part. At the end of the negotiations, the fate of six northern counties would remain unclear (*and it still is**) while Irish politicians would have to swear an oath of loyalty to the British crown.

In December 1921, independence was formally granted to the newly formed Irish state. The terms would prove too moderate for a minority at home, so the nation went to war against itself for nine months of extreme violence that traumatised large sections of society. In some homes, the Irish Civil War is still remembered, if at all, with a grimace.

Can we turn the page?

---

* *This is where Irish history gets even more divisive. In a respectable history of Dublin, this footnote would be four chapters. But you said you were busy?*

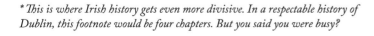

FOR MANY DUBLINERS, THE BENEFITS of Irish independence were largely symbolic. Leinster House was requisitioned to serve as a new parliament. *(Good.)* The red post-boxes were painted green. *(Grand.)* And the Catholic hierarchy soon exercised a firm hand on the delicate Irish mind. *(Hmm.*)* A great many things were cut, censored or banned, and in their rush to prevent the future, fanatical archbishops took control of essential health and education services. Meanwhile, politicians boasted about going to mass every day. Their deference was material as well as spiritual because the Free State government had almost no money.

Who else could possibly run all the hospitals and schools? Who had the necessary experience and authority?

---

* *The Catholic Church employed a lot of good men and women, and inspired millions of Irish people to live more virtuous lives. But it is also true that many vulnerable women and children were abused at the hands of the church. Was Ireland uniquely bad? The answer is still a subject of debate.*

CONVENT OF THE SACRED HEART. LR. LEESON STREET. DUBLIN

Lady Arabella Denny opened the first Magdalene asylum on Leeson Street in 1765. A Church of Ireland institution, it only accepted Protestant women. On the right, you can see a full-size replica of the Lourdes grotto... in Inchicore.

The National Museum, Dublin.

Civic pride demands that we show up for ourselves. For example, the front of Leinster House could serve as a great public piazza. It is, instead, a car park.

THE PROMISES OF THE REVOLUTION gave way to the tightass moralism of the Free State. Women saw their status reduced, the Irish Mammy became a byword for long-suffering, and many Dubliners decided to vote with their feet. Emigration is, and always has been, one Irish response to economic disaster.

But the early years of independence were also notable for something that did *not* happen. Unlike most other European countries, Ireland did not succumb to an extremist government of the far left or far right during the inter-war years. In the 1920s and 1930s, successive governments – whose leaders had fought a bitter war against each other, and often refused to be in the same room – managed to provide stability at a time of profound economic gloom. While it may seem strange to recognise something that did not happen, the significance of this achievement cannot be overstated.

WILLIAM BUTLER YEATS WON THE NOBEL PRIZE for Literature in 1923. The poet and senator devoted his prize to the new Free State. Here was the man who once wrote,

"I bring you with reverent hands
The books of my numberless dreams…"

Although he is linked with Sligo, Yeats kept returning to Dublin, unlike most of the city's great writers, such as George Bernard Shaw, James Joyce and Samuel Beckett, who made their lives overseas. At home or away, Dublin's writers made it a literary capital of the world. A place apart, not at ease with its surroundings, hated and misunderstood by many Irish people, Dublin has a lot of baggage, but its writers are peerless observers of the human condition. They put the city on the literary map, bringing people everywhere to a closer understanding of who they really are.

Today, Dublin is a UNESCO City of Literature.

WEST INDIES *v.* **IRELAND, College Park, Dublin, June 4th, 5th, 6th, 1928**

*Left to Right—Top Row—*E. A. RAE, F. R. MARTIN. J. A. SMALL, O. C. SCOTT, E. L. G. HOAD, M. P. FERNANDES. H. C. GRIFFITHS, L. S. CONSTANTINE, (Jun.) *Middle Row—*C. ROACH, C. V. WIGHT (*Vice-Capt.*), R. K. NUNES (*Capt.*) G. CHALLENOR, C. R. BROWNE. *Bottom Row—*G. FRANCIS. J. NEBLETT, E. L. BARTLETT, W. ST. HILL.

The West Indies cricket team played their first-ever test match at Lords in 1928. They warmed up with a game against Ireland in Trinity College. Unbeaten on the tour, the West Indies looked set to win, but with four minutes to spare, the home side captured the final wicket. A famous win for Ireland.

The Mansion House, Dublin.

Visitors to the Mansion House left with a box of Alfie-branded chocolates, and even when he said the wrong thing, it only added to his fame. He once promised to put shoes on the footless.

IN 1930, ALFIE BYRNE WAS ELECTED as the first Lord Mayor of Greater Dublin. He moved into the Mansion House on Dawson Street, and kept the title of Lord Mayor for the next nine years.* During that time, the slums were largely cleared, and 10,000 new homes were built in Dublin. This Home-Rule dinosaur would have you believe that he put the roof on every one of those houses.

Éamon de Valera got into government in 1932. Dev couldn't stand Alfie Byrne, but the over-dressed mayor was also a bridge-builder who had a paradoxical effect. He made the city smaller – "I know half of Dublin, and the other half knows me" – but also larger and more accommodating. Synonymous with courtesy and the plight of the poor, Byrne was a unique presence in the civic pageant. His nicknames included Alfred the Great, King Alfred, and the Shaking Hand of Dublin. By the end of his life, this odd little man was known everywhere as the Lord Mayor of Ireland.

*Alfie's son, Paddy Byrne, once told me that he grew up playing tennis in the back garden of the Mansion House.

THE FREE STATE REMAINED NEUTRAL in the Second World War. A temporary home to spies and glamorous refugees, Dublin was *almoſt* like the Casablanca of the north.

After the war, emigration and unemployment remained stubbornly high, and even after becoming a republic in 1949, the new Ireland continued to struggle. Dublin became the butt of all jokes and the source of all misery. Synonymous with the *ancien régime*, the city was nothing like the country it represented. In the absence of the English, it was an easy target.*

A place apart, Dublin remains an object of suspicion in Ireland, yet it is pleasantly different to Britain.

George Bernard Shaw's
Memorandum *from* GEORGE NEWNES, LIMITED.

TOWER HOUSE, SOUTHAMPTON STREET, STRAND,

LONDON, W.C.2.

TELEGRAMS: "NEWNES" RAND, LONDON. Ayot St Lawrence 9/1/ 1943
Welwyn, Herts.

~~Nothing doing~~. I never prophesy until I know; and nobody yet knows where those two will end.

[My best guess is that Adolf will enjoy a dignified retirement in the Vice-Regal Lodge in Dublin, which is presumably to let at present. ⟶ G. Bernard Shaw. ⟶

In 1943, the playwright George Bernard Shaw was asked when the Second World War would end. "Nothing doing. I never prophesy until I know; and nobody yet knows where those two [Churchill and Hitler] will end. My best guess is that Adolf will enjoy a dignified retirement in the Vice-Regal Lodge in Dublin, which is presumably to let at present."

C.P.O. & NELSON PILLAR DUBLIN

Dublin was not big enough to contain both subjects of this postcard. Architect Francis Johnston built the GPO *and* the Nelson Pillar. In 1966, three vandals blew up the Pillar. Today its position is occupied by a cold and heartless spike.

BETWEEN 1940 AND 1972, the archbishop of Dublin, John Charles McQuaid, doubled the footprint of the Catholic church, in an explosion of church and school building projects. Zealous to a fault, McQuaid even found time to rail against girls playing sport in skirts, because it might be impious. His heavy hand was felt all over Dublin.*

In 1959, a civil servant, T.K. Whitaker, told the *taoiseach* [prime minister] Seán Lemass that the national coffers were empty: it was time to open up the country to foreign investment. The economy jolted into life, and for the first time as the capital of a free nation, the city experienced a mini-boom.

In 1972, Ireland voted to join the European Economic Community; here was another seminal moment in the story of the nation. While the country's progress was far from constant, the experiment has exceeded the hopes of the most optimistic Europhile.

By the 1950s, the capital had the highest number of cinema seats per head of population of any city in Europe. Such was the clamour for escapism (though many films were censored). That Dublin is often characterised as a dour place. "If it sounds boring, it was," wrote Anthony Cronin. "If it sounds like living under the Taliban, it wasn't quite."

IN 1990, MARY ROBINSON WAS ELECTED as the first female president of Ireland. Her success in the role coincided with the emergence of a more affluent society. By the end of the twentieth century, Dublin felt like a gold-rush town in which the man who had the largest rock was the very pineapple of politeness.* In the heady years of the Celtic Tiger, *some* people spent money in the same carefree way that you might use shower gel in a friend's house.

For the first time in the history of the Irish state, a generation was not reared for export. *Or so it seemed.* The global financial crisis of 2008 revealed the shallow foundations of prosperity in Ireland, but also the resilience of its people. Because the sky did not fall in. The men from the International Monetary Fund were eventually seen off the premises, and foreign direct investment continued to support the cash-strapped Irish economy.

The pineapple of politeness? This is Mrs Malaprop in The Rivals *by Richard Brinsley Sheridan, who conquered the West End in 1775.*

Grafton Street, Dublin, Ireland.

Photo: P. O'Toole, John Hinde Studios.

A No. 10 bus drives down Grafton Street in this classic John Hinde postcard. The upmarket shopping street was pedestrianised in 1982. Switzers is on the right of the picture. In 1990, this elegant department store gave way to Brown Thomas, the spiritual home of the Celtic Tiger.

Dublin City and River Liffey, Ireland.

Photo: P. O'Toole, John Hinde Studios.

The postcards of Dublin are as colourful and quick to lie as your average Dublin character.

IN THE YEAR 2022, DUBLIN IS A SMALL, FRIENDLY, EXPENSIVE CITY. The only English-speaking capital in the European Union, it is home to the European headquarters of Facebook, LinkedIn and Google. At least a fifth of residents were born outside the state. (In the Little Museum, we think of Dublin as Europe's largest village.) Five million tourists visit the city in a normal year – and today, if they buy a postcard, it often serves as a cheap souvenir rather than as a means of communication.

In the digital age, there is a danger that humans may forget the charm of pen and ink. Writing a postcard is like putting out a press release from the person we want to become. So we turn on the sunshine. Some of us even pretend to enjoy a conference! We are like the exuberant colours of a John Hinde postcard.* In this sugar-coated vision, the photography reflects the aspirations of Dublin itself. *Here is the place we might yet become.*

In the Dictionary of Irish Biography, Hinde is described as someone who privileged the public good. For him, colour in photographs represented "optimism and vibrancy, and his desire to reproduce those qualities reflected his desire to promote the well-being of as large an audience as possible." This English postcard-entrepreneur made Ireland seem unusually glamorous.

W RITING A POSTCARD – and expecting it to be read without fear of reproach – these are among the gifts of freedom. We can speak our minds because we live in democracies. And the act of sending a postcard situates the correspondent and the recipient in a set of traditions that is at least 150 years old. But this is not just a story about the past.

Sometimes the airbrushed portrait of a city (*and so we return to the Green*) can be prophetic. Indeed, even the most anodyne image can reveal not simply who we are, or where we have come from, but who we may yet become. At peace, for example, with the rest of an island; at peace with our capital; at peace with the idea of beauty itself.

St. Stephen's Green,   DUBLIN.

Every picture contains within it the possibility of a completely
different future. If you look closely, you can see a city
museum emerging where it had no right to be.

UPPER O'CONNELL STREET, DUBLIN.

Back to the future at the Gresham Hotel on O'Connell St. Dublin is everywhere in these pictures, yet nothing is permanent. The figures were just passing through a frame. What does the city think of us?

F ALLING IN LOVE WITH A CITY is a lot easier than you might think. And tourists are particularly vulnerable. They can fancy a strange new place after a few hours of drunken applause. *But what does the city think of us?*

One answer is that we are fated to misunderstand each other. When we are young, the city is old, but when we are old, the place is so damn youthful! As citizens, we must try to enhance our surroundings, but at the end of our lives – or when we leave – Dublin might be just as happy to see the back of us.

Whatever the city thinks of you and me, we have good reason to admire its journey. For the Irish village that became a Viking town and an English city is today the capital of a hundred-year-old European republic.

And *that* is something to write home about.

Epilogue

CITIES ARE MORE FRAGILE than their critics allow. The truth is that humans are easily distracted. We let ourselves down. Sometimes we bounce back, of course, but our energy is not inexhaustible, we have limited powers of concentration, and there is nothing inevitable about progress. All this suggests a duty of tenderness: to ourselves, to each other, and to the planet. We have an obligation to be watchful.

In the eighteenth century, Jonathan Swift catalogued the moral failings of his age:

"[He] gave the little wealth he had,
To build a house for fools and mad:
And showed by one satiric touch,
No nation wanted it so much."

Swift asks us to provide a shelter for freedom. To make something more beautiful and more just than an ordinary city. To make history equal to the richness of Dublin.

Above all, he asks us to remain vigilant.

Acknowledgements

THIS HIGH SPEED HISTORY IS BOUND TO offend historians. *Oh dear!* The city of Dublin is well served by its biographers, and this publication relies on the research of so many good historians that it would be invidious to thank more than one: David Dickson, whose peerless history of the Irish capital is the perfect main course for anyone whose appetite is encouraged by this starter portion.

Many of the postcards in this catalogue were published a long time ago. Every effort has been made to identify copyright holders and obtain permission for the use of copyright material. Notification of any additions or corrections to be incorporated in future reprints or editions would be appreciated. Thanks to John Hinde Archive Ltd/John Hinde Collection, Rustington Museum Collection, Getty Images, Alamy, Shutterstock, the National Library of Ireland, the National Gallery of Ireland, Fáilte Ireland, the *Irish Times* and Ashley Van Haeften on Flickr for permission to reproduce images.

This publication was produced to coincide with an exhibition in the Little Museum of Dublin. It was made with assistance from the Heritage Council and our patrons in the Department of Tourism, Culture, Arts, Gaeltacht, Sport and Media. I am grateful to Virginia Teehan, Beatrice Kelly, Lesley-Ann Hayden, Amanda Ryan and Martina Malone in the Heritage Council; and to Minister Catherine Martin, Conor Falvey, Gerri O'Sullivan and Colm Lundberg in the Department of Tourism, Culture, Arts, Gaeltacht, Sport and Media.

Most of the images in this book are from the collections of the Little Museum of Dublin. This non-profit institution is housed in a building that is owned by our patrons in Dublin City Council. The museum is governed by a brilliant unpaid board whose members include our chair, Dr Rhona Mahony, and our treasurer, Brian Geraghty, as well as the Lord Mayor of Dublin, Councillor Mary Freehill, Councillor Hazel Chu, James Ryan, Catriona Crowe, Edward Brophy, Miriam Brady and Susan McKeon.

Much of this book was written in the Tyrone Guthrie Centre, Annaghmakerrig. This wonderful centre for artists and writers is supported by the Irish government.

I am grateful to Susan Jane and our boys, Benjamin and Marty. Last night, Marty (10) told me that Daniel O'Connell was a lawyer. He was impressed. I hope this work encourages Marty to learn more about O'Connell and other icons of Irish history, a subject that is not as lucrative as law, but much better for the heart.

I want to thank Leslie Stepp, Winter Romanov Hynes, Brody Sweeney, Lar Joye, Denis Hickie, Audrey Ryan, Mark McKenna, Marissa Wyll, Neil O'Donohoe and Fergal Tobin for reading the manuscript. The postcards were scanned by my colleague, Gintaras Varnagys. I am grateful to our design team, Dara Flynn and Barbara Sangster, who created this very handsome publication, as well as Sarah Clancy, Noeleen Murphy and all our team in the Little Museum, who bring humour and hospitality to the history of Dublin seven days a week. Finally, I also want to thank my colleagues Campbell Hannan and Daryl Hendley Rooney for proof-reading this book. Their assistance has been invaluable.

Any mistakes are, of course, the fault of the author alone.

Further Reading

Carey, Tim, *Dublin Since 1922*

Craig, Maurice, *Dublin 1660-1880: The Shaping of a City*

Crowe, Catriona, *Dublin 1911*

Daly, Mary E., *Dublin: The Deposed Capital*

Dickson, David, *Dublin: The Making of a Capital City*

Ferriter, Diarmaid, *The Transformation of Ireland 1900–2000*

Foster, R. F., *Modern Ireland, 1600–1972*

—, *Vivid Faces: The Revolutionary Generation in Ireland, 1890–1923*

Gibney, John, *A Short History of Ireland, 1500-2000*

Hegarty, Neil, *Dublin: A View from the Ground*

Kearns, Kevin C., *Dublin Street Life & Lore*

—, *Dublin Tenement Life: An Oral History*

Kelly, Deirdre, *Four Roads to Dublin*

Liddy, Pat, *Dublin: A Celebration*

McDonald, Frank, *A Little History of the Future of Dublin*

O'Brien, Jacqueline and Guinness, Desmond, *Dublin: A Grand Tour*

Somerville Large, Peter, *Dublin*

Sheehan, Ronan and Walsh, Brendan, *Dublin: The Heart of the City*

Tobin, Fergal, *The Irish Difference*

ONE OF THE "SMART SET."

copyright 1906
By The Rotograph Co. N.Y.

Trevor White was born in Dublin and refuses to leave. Former publisher of *The Dubliner* magazine, he is the author of six widely ignored books and founder of the Little Museum of Dublin. He lives in Rathmines with his wife, Susan Jane, their two children and a cat.

Notes *on the back of a postcard*